Politics, barbecue & balderdash

Editorial cartoons by

John Cole
The Herald-Sun

Extra-special thanks to the news and
editorial staffs of *The Herald-Sun*,
Publisher Rick Kaspar,
Executive Editor William E.N. Hawkins,
and to Cynthia,
John Sr. ("Man, you got perspicacity!"),
Beth, Fritz and Evinrude.

ISBN 0-9648472-0-5

Printed by Thomson-Shore Inc.,
Dexter, MI

In memory of Clark Mollenhoff,
who loved to catch them
with their pants down.

Management of *The Herald-Sun* would like to apologize in advance to anyone insulted by any of the cartoons in this book. In fact, management takes no responsibility for John Cole. After all, he is an adult – which makes it hard to explain why he takes Kentucky basketball seriously. In fact, it's the only thing he takes seriously.

Well, not quite. He takes his cartoons seriously. There are few things which can give a newspaper more personality than an editorial cartoonist who packs a punch, and *The Herald-Sun* is blessed with a great one. His cartoons, original and rich in detail, have started to attract national attention. This past year he was named one of North America's ten best in the annual Fischetti Competition in Chicago.

In this, his first collection of cartoons, you'll find John at point-blank range, hitting many of his favorite targets: politicians, gun nuts, criminals, hypocrites and, of course, tobacco companies. You figure out why his house reeks of cheap cigars.

And to all the callers I've heard from over the years who want to know "is John Cole sick or what?" I think this book will provide a clear answer.

Having been warned, turn the page and start laughing.

Bill Hawkins
Executive Editor, *The Herald-Sun*

While America chooses the least of three evils in the Presidential race,
North Carolinians choose between the lesser of two Jims (Hunt & Gardner) for Governor.

Bush struggles to show he is not a wimp, Clinton espouses Big Government,
and an eccentric midget billionaire plays the spoiler.

Bush seems paralyzed as the election approaches
amid an economic downturn.

Conservative (to be polite) columnist Pat Buchanan offers a more
potable message than former Klansman David Duke.

Bush and Clinton both attempt to tie themselves to Truman's legacy
by visiting the Truman Presidential Library.

NORTHERN EXPOSURE.

Meanwhile, convicted Iran-Contra felon Oliver North gives the old-line party
faithful heart palpitations in Virginia's Senatorial race.

Ross Perot exhibits a fondness for charts, homilies and some truly bizarre conspiracy theories

George Bush emerges from the 1992 GOP Convention armed for battle.
Well... sort of.

14

The N.C. Governor's race comes to a nasty end.
Jim Hunt wins, but it isn't pretty.

One of Hunt's closest political allies pleads guilty to eavesdropping on cellular phone calls by the Gardner campaign. Hunt pleads ignorance.

Bill Clinton wins, and immediately begins back-pedaling on the major themes of his campaign, setting the tone for the years to come

17

Clinton's first initiative — to lift the military's ban on gays — is coolly received by top brass who worry about unit cohesion and tight sleeping quarters for the enlisted men.

Clinton's bungled attempt to fire the White House travel staff (at the behest of a Hollywood pal) is derided by the GOP.

Clinton and his staff show a singular talent for
bungling nominations – Zoe Baird, Kimba Wood, Lani Guinier, Bobby Inman and Henry Foster.

With the White House in a state of disarray, Clinton brings in Washington insider and Durham native David Gergen to play Kindergarten Kop.

Clinton puts on a flight jacket and tours an aircraft carrier.
Nobody buys it.

THE OLD BALL AND CHAIN.

The Whitewater scandal calls Hillary Rodham Clinton's Little Rock law practice into question.
Bill maintains he was along for the ride.

South African President Nelson Mandela's wife becomes too much of a political liability. He fires her.
No such option on this side of the puddle.

Paula Jones files a sexual harassment suit –
chock-full of juicy details – against Bill Clinton.

On one issue after another, a weakened Clinton
caves in to outside pressure.

Clinton borrows a page from a previous White House occupant
following GOP gains in the 1994 elections

To mark the 50th anniversary of America's victory over Japan,
the administration suggests changing 'V-J Day' to 'End of the Pacific War.'

Senator Jesse Helms creates a furor when he opines that Clinton 'better bring a bodyguard' if he comes to North Carolina. Helms said he was joking. It's a joke even cartoonists don't use.

A series of threatening intrusions at The White House makes one wonder
why anyone would want to live there.

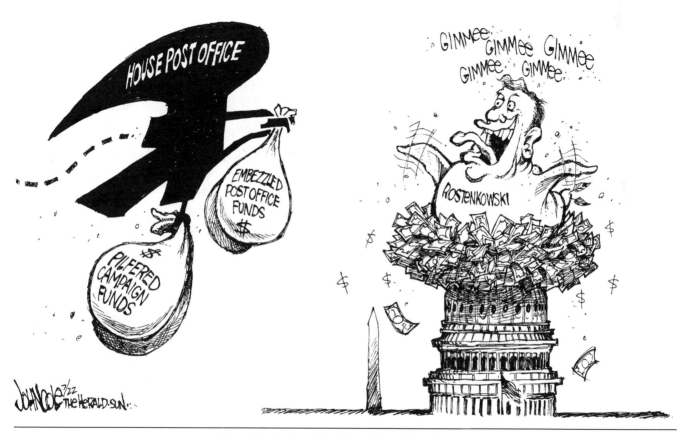

Wrongdoing in the U.S. House Post Office feathers
House Ways and Means Chairman's Dan Rostenkowski's nest.

Rostenkowski is indicted, later removed from his chairmanship,
and eventually thrown out of office by his constituents.

Clinton's reform package begins to look like the Birth of an Entitlement.

Clinton visits UNC as part of its 200th birthday bash

Senator Bob Dole administers the death blow to healthcare reform, using some procedural footwork, a filibuster, and more than a little help from conservative Democrats.

Tobacco growers resent government interference in their livelihood.

THE FIRST SIGN OF ADDICTION: DENIAL.

Tobacco executives, meanwhile, maintain under oath that nicotine is not addictive,
that tobacco is not harmful, and that the Earth is flat.

Liggett's own research indicates the company knew the dangers of smoking despite what executives said.

The tobacco industry and growers howl in protest at a proposed 75¢-a-pack tax on cigarettes.

Philip Morris discovers traces of 'potentially harmful' chemicals in its cigarette filters.

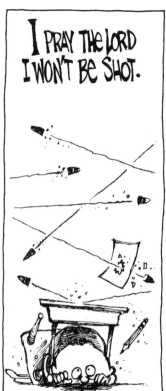

Guns are everywhere, even in the schoolyard.
Students could use a prayer.

America's fascination with firearms is disconcerting to many visitors. Japanese companies begin offering their employees training in how to cope with our workplace violence.

Politics in 1994 were heated, personal and, in many ways, contradictory.
Voters resent government intrusion, but still rely on it to address many basic needs.

A proposed postage stamp depicting the atomic bombing of Hiroshima draws the administration's ire.
Probably brought back memories of the past election.

Newly anointed House Speaker Newt Gingrich is one part college professor, one part revivalist and three parts pit bull. Cartoonists like him, if secretly.

"WELL, WELL... OUR FIRST CUSTOMER..."

One of the Speaker's proposals calls for the establishment of orphanages for poor and abused children. The Democrats seem to be in no position to argue the point.

Christmas comes to a changed Washington.

Republicans bring back block grants, starting with Clinton's anti-crime package

Newt labels the National Endowment for the Arts the 'sandbox of the cultural elite,' and aims to cut off it's funding. He might not know much about art, but he knows what he doesn't like.

As the GOP eyes everything from school lunch programs to welfare reform, the Democrats repeatedly evoke images of children starving in the streets.

OTHER TERM-LIMIT PROPOSALS...

"CONGRESS MEMBERS MAY SERVE AS LONG AS THEY LIKE, BUT ONLY IN THEIR UNDERWEAR AFTER THE THIRD TERM."

"A MAXIMUM OF FIVE TERMS, FOLLOWED BY A FIRING SQUAD."

READY... AIM...

THIS IS OVER THAT BRADY BILL VOTE... RIGHT?

"A CONSTITUTIONAL AMENDMENT MAKING IT ILLEGAL TO NOT VOTE."

WHAT? THAT'S (BELCH) UNAMERICAN!

AND NOW, BACK TO "RUSH"...

CHIPS

Republicans tried, and failed, to push through a Constitutional amendment for Congressional term limits.

Federal Reserve Chairman Alan Greenspan, fearing inflation from an overheated economy, repeatedly raises interest rates.

Martin Luther King Jr.'s heirs consult the keepers of Elvis' name on how to preserve and market the slain civil rights leader's legacy.

Newt's mom whispers it to CBS News' Connie Chung, who then trumpets it to the world.

Not to say there is no justice. Chung is dropped as CBS's co-anchor

Clinton's nomination of Dr. Henry Foster meets stiff GOP opposition
when it is learned he performed an uncertain number of abortions.

Where others have feared to tread, Foster decides to stand and fight.

"SORRY, DR. FOSTER, BUT WE HAVE TO ABORT THIS NOMINATION TO SAVE THE LIVES OF OUR CANDIDACIES."

Foster's nomination dies on the Senate floor,
victim of the presidential aspirations of Bob Dole and Phil Gramm.

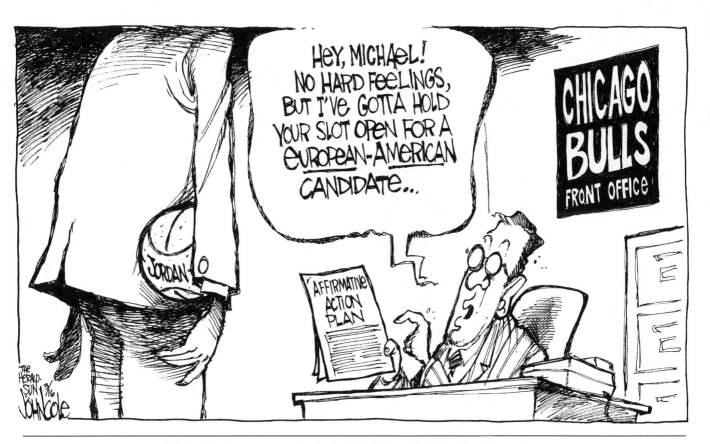

Michael Jordan returns to basketball. Politicians debate affirmative action.
Cartoonists put the two together.

59

Major League Baseball's strike cancels the World Series and threatens the 1995 season.
Clinton attempts to encourage a settlement. Fat chance.

Ross Perot weighs in on the debate over The North American Free Trade Agreement. $4 billion can give a man real relevancy, it seems.

Perot stumbles through a televised debate over NAFTA with V.P. Al Gore.
He seems unaccustomed to being disagreed with.

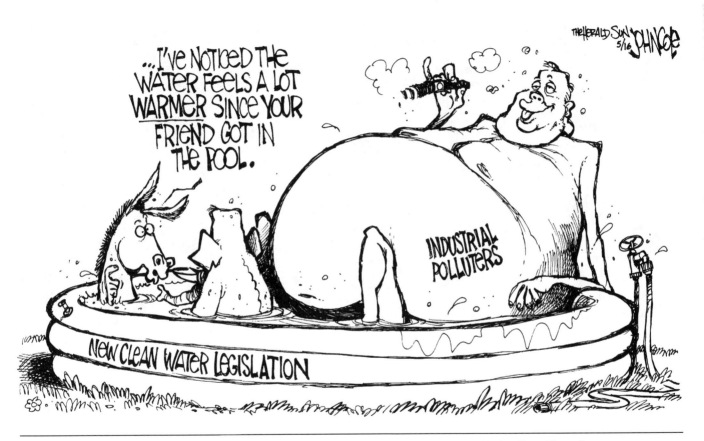

House Republicans begin to rewrite environmental regulations, beginning with the Clean Water Act.
They take their cues from industrial polluters.

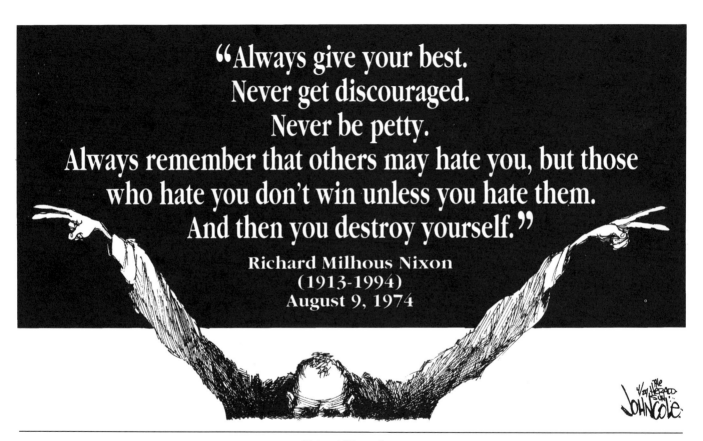

"Always give your best.
Never get discouraged.
Never be petty.
Always remember that others may hate you, but those
who hate you don't win unless you hate them.
And then you destroy yourself."

Richard Milhous Nixon
(1913-1994)
August 9, 1974

Richard Nixon dies
The quote is from his farewell address to the White House staff.

9:04 A.M., APRIL 19, OKLAHOMA CITY.

A bomb, apparently planted by right-wing fanatics, destroys the Alfred Murrah Building in Oklahoma City at 9:05 a.m.
A daycare center was housed on its bottom floor.

Newt and the seemingly eternal question.

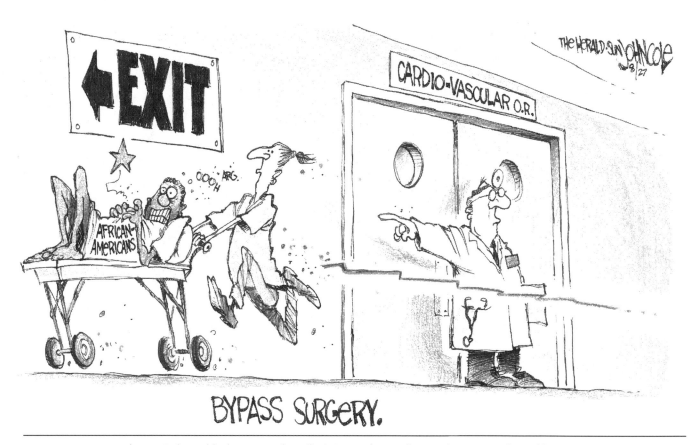

BYPASS SURGERY.

A report shows black men are less likely to receive cardiovascular surgery than white men.

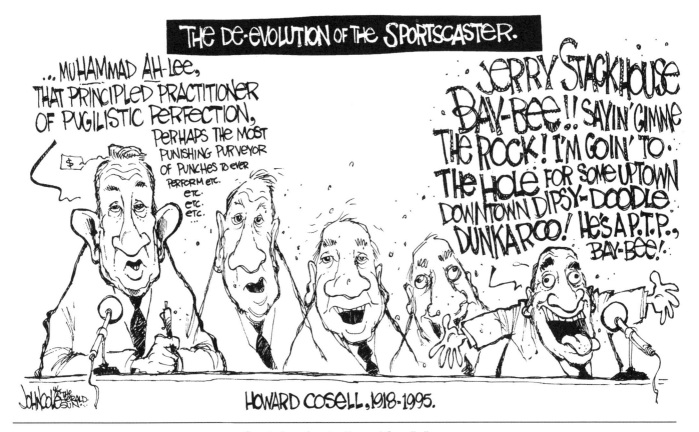

Sports broadcaster Howard Cosell dies.
Dick Vitale, however, roars on.

VLAD THE IMPALER.

Russian nationalist, neo-Nazi and professional party monster Vladimir Zhirinovsky
plans to build a better Russia on the backs of it ethnic minorities.

The Collapse of the Soviet Union unleashes a tide of ethnic warfare.
Leading that wave is Serbian President Slobodan Milosevic and his program of 'ethnic cleansing.'

NATO and the UN make empty threats. Serbs kill time, Muslims and Croats.

A U.S. fighter, part of NATO's peace-keeping forces, is shot down over Bosnia.
The pilot is later rescued.

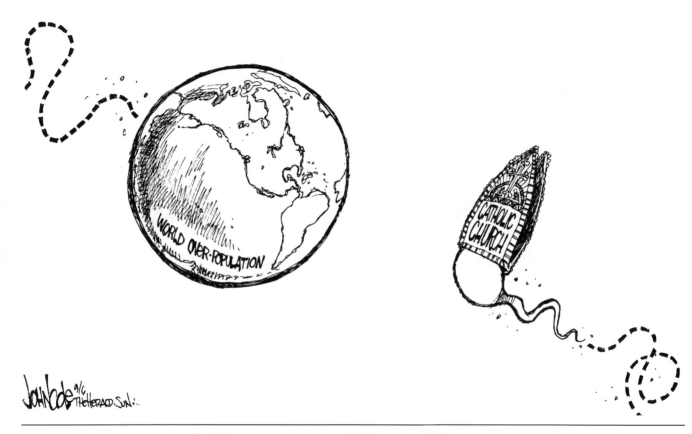

The Vatican opposes almost all birth-control initiatives during an
international conference on over-population.

Our good trading partners, the Chinese, have a
nasty practice of harvesting transplantable organs from their political prisoners.

Israel and the PLO sign an historic peace agreement.
Radical factions on both sides vow to destroy it.

Clinton tries to convince the public that restoring democracy in Haiti is worth the risk of American lives.

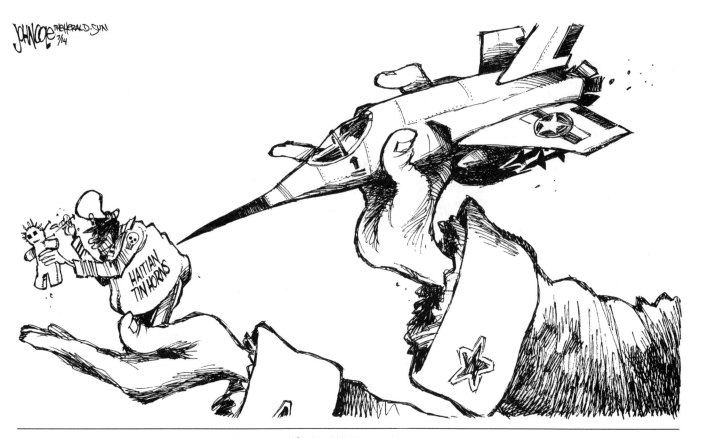

The audacity of Gen. Raoul Cedras' Haitian regime tests America's patience.

Jimmy Carter steps into the Haitian fray, averting a hostile American invasion.

Carter's Haitian effort undermines
Secretary of State Warren Christopher.

The lure of an American bailout for Mexico could prove costly to both parties.

Junior Senator Lauch Faircloth takes his cues from
North Carolina's elder, um, statesman, Jesse Helms.

Cost estimates for the new Durham Bulls ballpark come in way over budget,
hastening the departures of Councilman Chuck Grubb and Mayor Harry Rodenhizer.

One year late and millions over budget, Durham Bulls Athletic Park finally opens.
Those problems notwithstanding, the park is a gem.

The Bulls break in their new home by breaking the jaw of a Winston-Salem pitcher during a bench-clearing brawl on 'Stamp Out Domestic Violence Night' at DBAP.

© "Dean Smith"™, "UNC"™ and "The University of North Carolina"™ are property and registered trademarks of Nike Corporation. Unauthorized use is prohibited by contract and law.

Dean Smith signs a multi-million-dollar deal with Nike.
Academics wince.

Money magazine proclaims the Triangle (and Durham by inclusion)
as the nation's No. 1 place to live. Locals see their region as a curious choice.

Durham, Raleigh and Chapel Hill all claim to be the driving force
behind the Triangle's reputation.

Durham's murder rate hits a record.

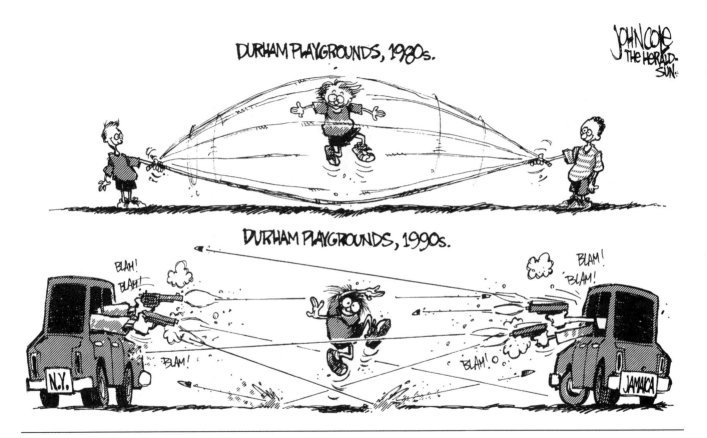

Durham kids get caught in the crossfire of drug dealers and other criminals

The mostly black Durham City Schools system is merged with the county system,
creating Durham's most contentious political struggle.

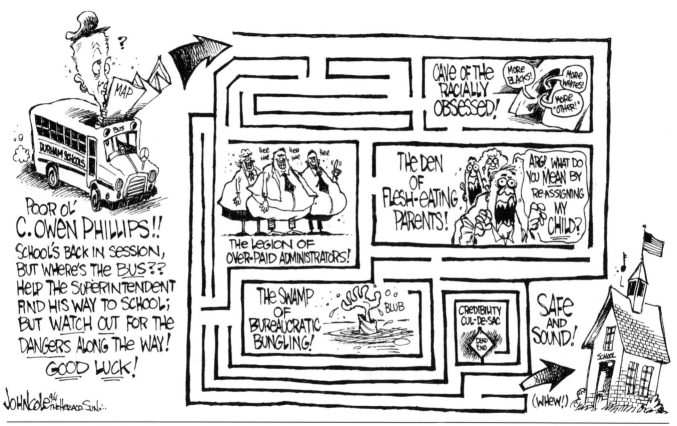

Durham's 1994-95 school year began with the collapse of the system's bus schedule, leaving many children stranded. This only added to Superintendent Phillips' student reassignment headaches.

Kids.
What do they know?

A gay film festival at the Carolina Theatre prompts calls for government action.
County Commissioners, however, have bigger fish to fry.

The Carolina Theatre finally opens its doors. Costly extravagances
virtually assure it won't stay open without government help.

Bill Bell's two decades of service on Durham County's Board of Commissioners comes to an end

Republicans Tommy Hunt and Ed DeVito strike fear into the hearts of county bureaucrats and workers.

Efforts to cut the county's payroll yield unwanted results.

Durham's child protection service finds itself short-handed with a heavy caseload.

The Saudi royal family rents two floors of Duke University Medical Center for two family members. Stories of lavish spending about town followed the visit, which Duke never confirmed.

Glaxo buys Burroughs Wellcome for $15 billion, merging two of RTP's biggest companies. Employees face an uncertain future.

A Chapel Hill High teacher offers his students a book containing dirty gay limericks.
Diversity marches on.

Condom distribution begins at Chapel Hill High School.

Wib Gulley's first intiative in the state Senate is to change the laws regarding bicyclists' hand signals.
Hey, its a law Durham can live with.

The state House of Representatives passes an array of tax cuts,
but leaves the 30-year-old, 'temporary' food tax in place.

Senator Faircloth (nor apparently the Senate Ethics Committee) wouldn't know a conflict of interest if it wore a name tag and bit him on the leg.

North Carolina's booming hog industry spreads its largess.
A 25,000,000-gallon hog-waste spill in Onslow County finally prompts action by Governor Jim Hunt.

Stock car driver and North Carolina icon Richard Petty contemplates a run for governor.

North Carolina death row inmate David Lawson wants his execution shown live on TV.
Phil Donahue jumps at the chance. The execution takes place sans cameras.

MERCEDES BEND.

Alabama gives away the farm to get the horse in its bid for a Mercedes-Benz plant.

KING JAMES VERSION

And God looked upon the earth, and, behold, it was corrupt; for all the flesh had corrupted His way upon the earth. And God said to Noah, "The end of all flesh is come before Me; for the earth is filled with violence through them; and, behold, I will destroy them with the earth."

BLACK BIBLE CHRONICLES VERSION

So the Almighty was hipped to what was going down... "I'm fed up, Noah, with what's happenin' 'round here. These folks ain't what's happenin' anymore, so I'm gonna do what I gotta do, and end things once and for all. Man, I'm gonna blow the brothers clean outta the water."

NEW BUBBA VERSION

Well, now, God took a gander at the earth, an' durned if'n He didn't get madder'n a wet hen. "Noah," he said, "ya'll been wallerin' around like a buncha idjits, an' y'all best believe I'm tired of foolin' with you. Now build that gol-dang boat, boy, 'fore I wear you out with this here tire iron."

The Black Bible Chronicles, written in urban black vernacular, is published.

A PC Trick or Treat.

The Wal-Marting of America.

Kids grow up too fast.

Di dumps Chuck.
Things have changed since Henry's day.

This just in: Fatty movie popcorn can kill you.

O.K. It was a slow news day.

An animal-rights activist tries to hit Ronald McDonald
with a cream pie at a local McDonald's.

Fossils of early dinosaurs are discovered in Research Triangle Park.

Born in Rochester, New York, and raised in Lexington, Kentucky, John Cole graduated in 1980 from Washington and Lee University. His newspaper career began in Greenup, Kentucky, covering local government and county-fair baby contests.

He joined the *Durham Morning Herald* and *The Durham Sun* in 1985 and, as Graphics Editor, oversaw the appearance and design of their merger into *The Herald-Sun.*

Cole lives in Durham, where he suffers with the Kentucky Wildcats, bangs on his guitar, enjoys a good cigar, and torments his cat, Evinrude.

HERALD-SUN PHOTO BY CATHY SEITH